# PARAGRAPH PRACTICE

*Prompts & Procedures to Practicing Paragraphs*

By Late November Learning Tree

PARAGRAPH PRACTICE
*PROMPTS AND PROCEDURES TO PRACTICING PARAGRAPHS*
BY LATE NOVEMBER LEARNING TREE

Published by Late November Literary
Winston Salem, NC 27107

ISBN: 979-8-9892723-2-7

Library of Congress Cataloging-in-Publication Data:
Late November Learning Tree.
Paragraph Practice / Late November Learning Tree 1st ed.

Printed in the United States of America

# TABLE OF CONTENTS:

# INTRODUCTION: POWERFUL PARAGRAPHS

Paragraph writing can often be a daunting task for young people. Coming up with an idea, and then formulating sentences around that idea is challenging when learning how to properly write and orally communicate. That's where this book comes in!

Paragraph Practice breaks down paragraph writing into easy steps. There are 10 sections in this book all designed to make paragraph writing easy to master. Practice prompts are provided, along with a section to practice paragraph editing. By the end of this book, your student will be writing powerful paragraphs and will be ready to move forward in their writing.

What makes a powerful paragraph? The simple answer is this: one supported thought or idea. A powerful paragraph doesn't have to be long or wordy. It shouldn't lose focus, but instead, it offers support to the overarching idea.

# PARAGRAPH PRACTICE:

# PREPARING

# CHECK FOR UNDERSTANDING

**Please answer these questions based on your prior knowledge. Complete your answers before you begin this workbook. It will help you understand what you already know versus what you need to learn.**

1. What is the topic sentence in a paragraph?

   _____

2. Where should a topic sentence go?

   _____

3. What is a paragraph?

   _____

4. How many sentences should be in a paragraph?

   _____

5. What are supporting sentences in a paragraph?

   _____

6. Is this a good paragraph? Yes, or no? Please explain your answer.

   The best dessert to have on your birthday is cake. Everyone likes ice cream but not me. Ice cream gives me a headache. It hurts my teeth. I don't like to eat it.

   _____

   _____

# THE MAKING OF A PARAGRAPH

- A good paragraph should be around five-to-seven sentences long.

- A good paragraph should focus on one topic.

- A good paragraph should follow this pattern:

  o *Topic Sentence:*

  My favorite thing to do in the summer is sleep in late.

  o *Supporting Sentence:*

  During the school year, I must wake up before 6 a.m. to catch the school bus, which is exhausting.

  o *Supporting Sentence:*

  Research shows that young people need more than eight hours of sleep a night.

  o *Supporting Sentence:*

  Getting a good night's sleep is simply hard to do when I wake up early in the school year.

  o *Closing Sentence:*

  For these reasons, sleeping in during the summer is a high priority for me.

# PARAGRAPH PREPARATION

**Tackling the Topic Sentence:**

Topic Sentences are the show starters when it comes to paragraphs. Here's what you need to know:

- Topic Sentences are statements. They are not questions.

- Topic Sentences are the first sentence of a paragraph.

- Topic Sentences inform the reader about the general idea of the paragraph.

## What would make a good topic sentence for this paragraph?

Read the paragraph below and select from the choices which topic sentence best works for the overall idea of the paragraph. Circle the answer and write it in the blank to complete the paragraph.

_____. The sun is out and stays in the sky until late in the evening. The days are warm, which makes it perfect swimming weather. Then there are the cookouts, bonfires, camping, and popsicles to enjoy! Last, but most importantly, there is no school. The days are mine to do whatever I please. What's not to love about summer?

    A. Doing what I want is important to me.

    B. Summer is my favorite season.

    C. Sunny days are better than cloudy days.

    D. Swimming is the best summer sport.

*The correct answer is (B). The entire paragraph discusses several ways that summer is a great season. Since that is the overall idea of the paragraph, selection (B) best fits with that idea.*

4

# What would make a good topic sentence for this paragraph?

Read the paragraph below and select from the choices which topic sentence best works for the overall idea of the paragraph. Circle the answer and write it in the blank to complete the paragraph.

_____. There is an amazing feast that's prepared. My mom makes the best mashed potatoes, my aunt brings her delicious pies, and my dad and uncle know how to perfectly fry the turkey. The best part is I get to spend the whole day with my cousins who live far away. Even though I like other holidays, Thanksgiving is special because it's not a day focused on gifts and materialism, but it's a day that simply focuses on being thankful.

    A.  The best part of any holiday is the food.

    B.  Thanksgiving is better than Christmas.

    C.  Thanksgiving is the best holiday of the year.

    D.  Thanksgiving is not about gift-giving.

*The correct answer is (C). The entire paragraph discusses several ways that Thanksgiving is a great holiday. Since that is the overall idea of the paragraph, selection (C) best fits with that idea.*

# What would make a good topic sentence for this paragraph?

Read the paragraph below and write the topic sentence that you feel best states the general idea of the paragraph.

_____. Some families choose to send their children to private schools. This option often is an expense upon the parents, but they see it as investment toward good education. Other families may choose to school their children at home. This option is not as much a financial burden, but it does take up a lot of the parents' time in terms of teaching and lesson planning. Most families choose to put their children in public school where it is cost-friendly and time-efficient. Each family is different and choosing the best schools for their children is an important freedom to have.

# IT'S TIME FOR PARAGRAPH PRACTICE!

**Write a strong five-sentence paragraph that answers this question:**
*What is your favorite holiday?*
**Your topic sentence should answer the question, and the rest of the paragraph should support the topic sentence with reasons why.**

## Example paragraph:

My favorite holiday is the fourth of July. This is my favorite because it is where we celebrate our country's independence. I like it because it is in the summer, and my family always rents a boat and has fun at the lake. There are fireworks at the end of the day, and they are spectacular. These are some reasons why my favorite holiday is the fourth of July.

### YOUR TURN

*Topic Sentence:*

_____

*Supporting Sentence:*

_____

*Supporting Sentence:*

_____

*Supporting Sentence:*

_____

*Closing Sentence:*

_____

# IT'S TIME FOR PARAGRAPH PRACTICE!

**Write a strong five-sentence paragraph that answers this question:**
*Which family pet is better: dogs or cats?*
**Your topic sentence should answer the question, and the rest of the paragraph should support the topic sentence with reasons why.**

## Example paragraph:

Dogs and cats make great family pets, but cats are slightly better. Cats take care of themselves, which helps busy families. Cats are also a lot quieter than dogs. Dogs will bark and bark, but cats keep to themselves. Even though cats are more independent than dogs, they still show affection and have funny antics. Dogs may make great family pets, but cats are better for busy families.

## YOUR TURN

*Topic Sentence:*

_____

*Supporting Sentence:*

_____

*Supporting Sentence:*

_____

*Supporting Sentence:*

_____

*Closing Sentence:*

_____

# IT'S TIME FOR PARAGRAPH PRACTICE!

**Write a strong five-sentence paragraph that answers this prompt:**
*If I could get tickets to one major sporting event, this would be it.*

## Example paragraph:

If I could get tickets to one major sporting event, it would have to be the Superbowl. The Superbowl is more than just a football game. It's a culmination of the season's best two football teams facing off in what is an epic American tradition. This is also a heavily anticipated concert with some of the best performers taking the stage in the middle of the field during half-time. For these reasons, I would love to attend the Superbowl just once.

### YOUR TURN

*Topic Sentence:*

_____

*Supporting Sentence:*

_____

*Supporting Sentence:*

_____

*Supporting Sentence:*

_____

*Closing Sentence:*

_____

# IT'S TIME FOR PARAGRAPH PRACTICE!

**Write a strong five-sentence paragraph that answers this prompt:**
*If I could go back in time, this is where I would go and what I would do.*

## Example paragraph:

Going back in time would be interesting, especially if I could go back to when my parents were teenagers. I would want to meet them and see what they did for fun. It would also be funny to see what trouble they got themselves into! I could get to see my grandparents again because they both passed away when I was younger. I would give everyone a big hug and tell them that I came from the future. Their expressions would be priceless!

### YOUR TURN

*Topic Sentence:*

_____

*Supporting Sentence:*

_____

*Supporting Sentence:*

_____

*Supporting Sentence:*

_____

*Closing Sentence:*

_____

# IT'S TIME FOR PARAGRAPH PRACTICE!

**Write a strong five-sentence paragraph that answers this prompt:**
*If I was stranded on a deserted island with only three items, this is what they would be and why.*

## Example paragraph:

If I only got to have three items to help me survive on an island, they would be a tarp, a flint to start fires, and a large canteen full of water. The most important reason why I choose these items is because it's all about survival. A tarp would help in creating a shelter. A flint would help me keep warm, cook fish, as well as alerting those looking for me of my location. A canteen full of water is a must because we can't drink salt water. If I could have one more item, it would be a pocketknife or axe. These are the things I'd want with me.

### YOUR TURN

*Topic Sentence:*

_____

*Supporting Sentence:*

_____

*Supporting Sentence:*

_____

*Supporting Sentence:*

_____

*Closing Sentence:*

_____

# PARAGRAPH PRACTICE: INFORMING

# IT'S TIME FOR PARAGRAPH PRACTICE!

**Write a strong five-sentence paragraph that *informs* the reader about something at which you excel. Are you good at games or singing? Are you good at cooking or being a helper?**

## Example paragraph:

Making the perfect grilled cheese takes practice. I first learned how to make grilled cheese from my mother. First, we use thick slices of white bread and two pieces of Velveeta melty cheese. Next, we spread melted butter on two slices of bread. This will make the bread nice and crispy once grilled. It is important to preheat the pan on medium heat, which makes the grilled cheese perfect. I am good at making grilled cheese.

## YOUR TURN

_____

_____

_____

_____

_____

_____

_____

_____

# IT'S TIME FOR PARAGRAPH PRACTICE!

**Write a strong five-sentence paragraph that *informs* the reader about a certain American president. Feel free to research information about him before writing your paragraph.**

## Example paragraph:

Abraham Lincoln had one of the most difficult presidencies in our nation's history. He became president in 1861 and struggled to keep peace between the southern and northern states. When the south unified and declared secession due to their refusal to give up slavery, Lincoln saw it as illegal and threatened federal action. This ultimately cost over 600,000 American lives. From Lincoln's humble beginnings to his perpetual struggle in his presidency, he is now a respected national leader in our country's archives for helping change the course of our nation.

### YOUR TURN

_____

_____

_____

_____

_____

_____

_____

# IT'S TIME FOR PARAGRAPH PRACTICE!

**Write a strong five-sentence paragraph that *informs* the reader about the effects of smoking tobacco products. Feel free to research information before writing the paragraph.**

## Example paragraph:

Smoking cigarettes is harmful to your body, and it hurts others around you. First, it damages your lungs and even your blood vessels. Research shows that it causes many types of diseases such as lung and skin cancers. Not only does smoking affect you as a smoker, but it hurts those around you. Second-hand smoke can be deadly too. It's important to stay informed about the negative effects of smoking.

## YOUR TURN

_____

_____

_____

_____

_____

_____

_____

# IT'S TIME FOR PARAGRAPH PRACTICE!

**Write a strong five-sentence paragraph that *informs* the reader about ways to stay healthy. Feel free to research information before writing the paragraph.**

## Example paragraph:

Staying healthy is a must to live a long, vibrant life, and there are tried and true ways to accomplish this. The first step to staying healthy is to make sure you eat a healthy diet. Fruits, vegetables, and protein are considered healthy while soda, chips, and desserts are not considered healthy. Another step to a healthy lifestyle is keeping active. It is not healthy to sit all day and not get your heart rate up and your blood pumping. These steps will help you be healthy.

## YOUR TURN

_____

_____

_____

_____

_____

_____

_____

# IT'S TIME FOR PARAGRAPH PRACTICE!

**Write a strong five-sentence paragraph that *informs* the reader about national parks to visit. Feel free to research information before writing the paragraph.**

## Example paragraph:

In the United States, there are 63 national parks, and each of them should be visited at least once with these two making the top of the list. The first national park to be visited is Redwood National Park in California. The sheer size and beauty of the trees is reason enough to explore. The second national park worthy of a visit is Yellowstone, located in Wyoming. It is the oldest national park and has spouting hot water and other fun land features and oddities. Whichever national park you desire to visit, you will enjoy the breathtaking splendor of our nation's forests and lands.

### YOUR TURN

_____

_____

_____

_____

_____

_____

_____

# PARAGRAPH PRACTICE: PERSUADING

# IT'S TIME FOR PARAGRAPH PRACTICE!

**Write a strong five-sentence paragraph that *persuades* the reader to support your stand/opinion on this topic: *Should there be time limits on video games?***

## Example paragraph:

There are several reasons why we should not have time limits on media or games. First of all, students have to complete their schoolwork, and there is a lot to do during the day. Our brains are learning information, and it is important that we have down time to relax in our way. Also, if we have completed our chores and our schoolwork, it does not make sense to limit our relaxation time. We need to unwind too.

### YOUR TURN

_____

_____

_____

_____

_____

_____

_____

# IT'S TIME FOR PARAGRAPH PRACTICE!

**Write a strong five-sentence paragraph that *persuades* the reader to support your stand/opinion on this topic: *Should the driving age be changed from 16 to 18?***

## Example paragraph:

There are several reasons why the driving age should be changed to 18. First of all, young people are already too busy with life and events to have to add driving to their list of responsibilities. Secondly, young drivers get in more accidents because they become easily distracted, and they haven't had years of practice. Young people may want their freedom, but driving is a major responsibility and will raise the family's car insurance. For these reasons, the driving age should be changed to 18.

## YOUR TURN

_____

_____

_____

_____

_____

_____

# IT'S TIME FOR PARAGRAPH PRACTICE!

**Write a strong five-sentence paragraph that *persuades* the reader to support your stand/opinion on this topic: *Should schools require uniforms?***

## Example paragraph:

Schools should require uniforms for several reasons. Some of the current styles are distracting and can even be immodest. When there are school uniforms, all the students will not have to worry about who is wearing what. Instead, they can focus on their classes. Many kids already do not take school seriously. They think it's a place to just hang out with friends. School uniforms would make school more professional and maybe kids would take it more seriously.

## YOUR TURN

_____

_____

_____

_____

_____

_____

_____

# IT'S TIME FOR PARAGRAPH PRACTICE!

Write a strong five-sentence paragraph that *persuades* the reader to support your stand/opinion on this topic: *Should the voting age in the U.S. be lowered to 16?*

## Example paragraph:

There are many reasons why the voting age should not be lowered to 16. Young people are notorious for making rash decisions and to be bad risk-takers. They are still learning about the world and about who they are. Voting is an important right, and it should be taken seriously. Giving teens a chance to grow up and to get a better understanding of the world is best.

## YOUR TURN

_____

_____

_____

_____

_____

_____

_____

# IT'S TIME FOR PARAGRAPH PRACTICE!

**Write a strong five-sentence paragraph that *persuades* the reader to support your stand/opinion on this topic: *Should junk food be banned from all schools?***

## Example paragraph:

Junk food is not good for anyone, and it should not be sold in schools. First, eating junk food creates a bad habit. Research shows that sugar is addictive, which means the more a person eats it, the more they want it. It doesn't make sense to push this type of bad habit on students. Would schools sell cigarettes? If this is an absurd question, then it should be just as absurd to sell junk food to the students. Schools should always promote health.

### YOUR TURN

_____

_____

_____

_____

_____

_____

_____

# IT'S TIME FOR PARAGRAPH PRACTICE!

**Write a strong five-sentence paragraph that *persuades* the reader to support your stand/opinion on this topic: *Should school be year-round?***

## Example paragraph:

Adults probably think that year-round school is a good thing, but students most likely disagree. The reason they may disagree is because school is hard, and taking breaks from academics help a student's mental health. As students get older, they may want summer jobs, and school would get in the way of that. Ultimately, students deserve to take a break and enjoy the sunshine and fresh air of summer. It shouldn't be taken away from them.

## YOUR TURN

# IT'S TIME FOR PARAGRAPH PRACTICE!

**Write a strong five-sentence paragraph that *persuades* the reader to support your stand/opinion on this topic: *Should homework be abolished?***

## Example paragraph:

Teachers may think homework is a good thing and needed, but students and parents often say it's not. Homework can be frustrating for a lot of children who struggle to understand it, which puts pressure on the parent to teach the material. Sometimes school projects can take hours, giving no free time to the students. With families' busy schedules, homework is a task that doesn't make sense. What is taught in school should stay in school.

## YOUR TURN

_____

_____

_____

_____

_____

_____

_____

# PARAGRAPH PRACTICE: REFLECTING

# IT'S TIME FOR PARAGRAPH PRACTICE!

**Write a strong five-sentence paragraph that *reflects* on this thought:**

*I am grateful...*

## Example paragraph:

I am grateful for many things. First, I am grateful for my parents. They work hard to give us a good life and take us to do fun things. I am also grateful for our dog, Lucy. She is a good listener and cuddler, and I love her. Third, my music means a lot to me, and I am grateful for it. I listen to music all the time and sing, and I am also learning the guitar. These are just a few things for which I am grateful.

## YOUR TURN

_____

_____

_____

_____

_____

_____

_____

# IT'S TIME FOR PARAGRAPH PRACTICE!

**Write a strong five-sentence paragraph that *reflects* on this thought:**

*I am hopeful...*

## Example paragraph:

I am hopeful for many things. First, I have hope that if I treat people with kindness that they would respond and treat others with kindness. I also hope that our nation will learn to appreciate the things that make us different and not to judge each other because of these differences. In my personal life, I am hopeful to become a better soccer player and to be an important part of a winning team. These are some of the things of which I am hopeful.

## YOUR TURN

_____

_____

_____

_____

_____

_____

_____

# IT'S TIME FOR PARAGRAPH PRACTICE!

**Write a strong five-sentence paragraph that *reflects* on this thought:**

*This brings me joy...*

## Example paragraph:

There are many things that bring me joy, and there are certain people who bring me joy too. When I am spending time with my cousins during the holidays, it brings me a lot of joy. I am also joyful when I get along with my siblings and we're not arguing all the time. My parents and grandparents do a lot of nice things for us, and it really does create joy in the family. Lastly, lazy summer days by the pool bring me joy because it's relaxing and a fun time with friends. Overall, life is joyful when you let it be.

### YOUR TURN

_____

_____

_____

_____

_____

_____

_____

# IT'S TIME FOR PARAGRAPH PRACTICE!

**Write a strong five-sentence paragraph that *reflects* on this thought:**

*God is great...*

## Example paragraph:

I am often overwhelmed by the greatness of God. I see him in so many things, such as in nature and when people are helping others. One way I see the greatness of God is when I go camping with my family, and we all stare up at the stars. To think that the galaxy is so huge and that there are galaxies upon galaxies makes me feel very small, yet God loves me and knows me by name. It always warms my heart, and it makes me in awe of his greatness.

### YOUR TURN

_____

_____

_____

_____

_____

_____

_____

# IT'S TIME FOR PARAGRAPH PRACTICE!

**Write a strong five-sentence paragraph that *reflects* on this thought:**

*My strengths...*

## Example paragraph:

I may be good at certain things, like playing the guitar or playing soccer, but my strengths are different. My first strength is that I'm loyal to my family and friends. I will defend them and not talk bad about them. Another strength is that I don't mind helping my mother with the chores. I actually don't mind putting away the dishes or vacuuming. My mother says I am thoughtful, so I consider that a strength.

### YOUR TURN

_____

_____

_____

_____

_____

_____

_____

# IT'S TIME FOR PARAGRAPH PRACTICE!

**Write a strong five-sentence paragraph that *reflects* on this thought:**

*My challenges...*

## Example paragraph:

There are certain things that are a challenge to me. For example, I struggle to understand math. I try and eventually I understand basic concepts, but it feels as if my brain is not wired to explore math. Another challenge of mine is that I'm impatient. I don't like waiting in line or being stuck in traffic. That leads to another challenge, and that is I spout out in anger too fast. If I'm annoyed, anyone in the room will hear about it. I understand that these are challenges in my life, and I need to grow and improve myself.

## YOUR TURN

_____

_____

_____

_____

_____

_____

_____

# PARAGRAPH PRACTICE: SUMMARIZING

# IT'S TIME FOR PARAGRAPH PRACTICE!

Summarize your favorite children's movie in 5-7 sentences:

## Example Paragraph:

On the streets of Acrabah lives a poor guy, named Aladdin, who steals just to get by. It's there he meets the princess, Jasmin, who left the stifling security of the palace to experience the world. When she is sent back home, Aladdin is desperate to see her again but knows that he doesn't have a chance. Luckily for him, Jafar needs someone to enter the cave of wonders and retrieve a powerful lamp. Aladdin is successful, but Jafar double-crosses him. It's then Aladdin meets the genie from the lamp. The genie helps Aladdin become a prince, and Aladdin promises to use his last wish to set the genie free. After some tricky situations with Jafar, Aladdin defeats Jafar for good, tells the truth to Jasmin, and wishes the genie free.

## YOUR TURN

_____

_____

_____

_____

_____

_____

# IT'S TIME FOR PARAGRAPH PRACTICE!

Summarize the steps and/or rules to your favorite sport in 5-7 sentences.

## Example Paragraph:

Competitive swimming is anything but easy. First, a person must learn how to swim, how to hold their breath underwater, and lastly, how to swim with speed. There are several types of strokes that swimmers must learn: freestyle, backstroke, butterfly, and breaststroke. Competitive swimming involves using your entire body to move quickly through the water following the specific stroke pattern for that race. Swimmers competing line up on their assigned block and take their initial stance. When they hear the starting whistle or horn, the race begins! They dive into the water and swim from one end of the pool to the other. Competitive swimming is exhilarating and fun!

## YOUR TURN

_____

_____

_____

_____

_____

_____

_____

# IT'S TIME FOR PARAGRAPH PRACTICE!

Summarize your personality and character traits in 5-7 sentences. What makes you...*you?*

## Example Paragraph:

There are many personality traits to me that make me unique. First of all, I am a quiet personality at first, but once someone gets to know me, I am bubbly and friendly. Not only am I quiet when first in a new situation, but I'm also observant. I like to study things out and see what's what and who's who. Some people may think I'm shy, but I'm really not. I merely like to know a situation before I share myself. One quirky thing about me is that I memorize movie lines. There are hundreds in my brain, and I can pull them out at random times. These attributes are a few of what makes me...*me.*

### YOUR TURN

_____

_____

_____

_____

_____

_____

_____

# IT'S TIME FOR PARAGRAPH PRACTICE!

Summarize the last book or short story you read (or your favorite book of all time) in 5-7 sentences.

## Example Paragraph:

The last short story I read was for class. It's called, "The Most Dangerous Game." In the story, there is a skilled hunter named Rainsford who unexpectedly falls off a yacht in the night. He swims to a small island that has a bad reputation, but he has no choice. He stumbles upon a large mansion and is introduced to General Zaroff. He is invited to dinner, and Zaroff tells him that he hunts dangerous prey. When Rainsford realizes it's men that Zaroff hunts, it's too late. Zaroff has decided that he will hunt Rainsford. The rest of the story is a game of cat-and-mouse where Rainsford runs for his life while trying to outsmart Zaroff. He eventually is successful by jumping off a cliff, swimming to shore, and hiding in Zaroff's room.

### YOUR TURN

_____

_____

_____

_____

_____

_____

_____

# IT'S TIME FOR PARAGRAPH PRACTICE!

Summarize a funny family story in 5-7 sentences that's happened either recently or in years gone by.

## Example Paragraph:

My grandpa likes to tell the story of his brother getting stuck in a snowbank. My grandpa and his brother decided to take their father's Buick out for a spin and do some donuts in the church parking lot by their house. They argued over who should drive, but neither had their license yet. My grandpa drove first, and he managed the car just fine. When his brother took over, he lost control, and the car spun out and slid into a snowbank. They couldn't get it out and had to walk the whole way home, wake up their father, and get help. My grandpa tells this story all the time that he should have never let his brother drive.

## YOUR TURN

_____

_____

_____

_____

_____

_____

_____

# IT'S TIME FOR PARAGRAPH PRACTICE!

Summarize what a typical day for you looks like in 5-7 sentences.

## Example Paragraph:

A typical day for me isn't too exciting. First, it takes me awhile to wake up. I'm definitely not an early bird. Thankfully, I homeschool, and my mom doesn't make me start schoolwork until 10 a.m. Once I'm awake though, I'm motivated to get my schoolwork done. I have a system. My first subject is math because I want to get that out of the way. Then I jump into science and then history. I make a game of it to see if I can finish those subjects before lunch. Sometimes I do, but sometimes I don't. After lunch, it's reading time and then an online writing class. Once my schoolwork is done, I either have piano lessons or swim practice. In the evenings, I get to chill and play video games or watch some television. It may not be super exciting, but I like my routine.

## YOUR TURN

_____

_____

_____

_____

_____

_____

_____

# IT'S TIME FOR PARAGRAPH PRACTICE!

Summarize what a perfect vacation would be for you in 5-7 sentences.

## Example Paragraph:

A perfect vacation starts and ends at the beach. It begins with renting a nice house or condominium on the water. Ocean front would be ideal. From there, the weather would be warm but not too hot. My perfect vacation wouldn't include a lot of activities because I'm happy sitting on the beach with a good book. However, going out to different restaurants and trying new cuisines is a must for the best vacation. Ice cream cones and leisurely walks along the surf would be a daily occurrence. This nicely summarizes my perfect vacation.

### YOUR TURN

_____

_____

_____

_____

_____

_____

_____

_____

# IT'S TIME FOR PARAGRAPH PRACTICE!

Summarize what you would need to have a great camping experience with friends or family in 5-7 sentences.

## Example Paragraph:

There are certain items that a camper needs to make it a fun, relaxing experience with friends. The two most important categories are shelter and food. Having a tent or two, along with proper bedding, is a must. Having a cooler and bin with food and proper utensils and tools is next on the list. Even if campers decide to live off the land, it is better to be safe with food supplies, then to not have anything. After these two essential categories are taken care of, it's important to be in a great location for camping, specifically one that is close to nature with proper equipment, such as picnic tables and fire pits. Lastly, a camper needs a change of clothes and a change of shoes. If all these categories are met, a great camping experience can be had by all.

## YOUR TURN

_____

_____

_____

_____

_____

_____

_____

# IT'S TIME FOR PARAGRAPH PRACTICE!

Summarize the traits of a person you admire in 5-7 sentences. This person can be someone you know, or a celebrity, or even a fictional character.

## Example Paragraph:

There are several successful businesswomen that I look up to and admire. They have certain traits that I desire to have in my own life so that I too can be successful. First, these women did not allow negative circumstances to deter them from their goals. Second, these women are smart and are not intimidated by others. Third, these women have taken chances in their lives, resulting in some failures but in other major successes. I've learned through them that you have to dream big and work hard to be successful.

## YOUR TURN

_____

_____

_____

_____

_____

_____

_____

_____

# IT'S TIME FOR PARAGRAPH PRACTICE!

Summarize the directions of your favorite game in 5-7 sentences to someone who has never played it. (This can be a board game or a video game).

## Example Paragraph:

If someone wants to play the dice game, *You Blew It,* they need to understand the rules. First, each player takes a turn rolling seven dice. They need to earn at least 500 points to get on the board, and that can only be done rolling ones or fives or three of a kind. If a player rolls a one, they earn 100 points. If they roll a five, they earn 50 points. If they roll three of a kind, they place two zeroes behind the number. So, if they rolled three sixes, they would earn 600 points. When a player rolls three ones, they hit the jackpot and earn 1,000 points. The game of dice is fun and competitive and can last as long as the players want. The winner earns the most points.

### YOUR TURN

_____

_____

_____

_____

_____

_____

_____

# PARAGRAPH PRACTICE:

# CREATIVE PARAGRAPHS

# IT'S TIME FOR PARAGRAPH PRACTICE!

**Write a strong five-sentence *creative* paragraph that tells a magical story.**

## Example paragraph:

Once upon a time, there was a boy with blue hair, named Billy. His blue hair had the special ability to make it snowy and cold. The townspeople were afraid of him because they liked summer, so they locked him in the tallest tower of a faraway castle. He became lonely, then sad, and then mad. As he grew up, he turned the tower to ice and smashed it down with a hammer. He was determined to destroy the town where he came from, but he met a girl who thawed his heart. They fell in love.

## YOUR TURN

_____

_____

_____

_____

_____

_____

_____

_____

# IT'S TIME FOR PARAGRAPH PRACTICE!

**Write a strong five-sentence *creative* paragraph that tells a sports story.**

## Example paragraph:

Lily liked to run in long-distance races, and today was the day of the state championship. She wasn't supposed to wake up with a sharp pain in her ankle, but that's exactly what happened. She tried to walk on it, but it hurt too badly. When her mother yelled up the stairs for her to hurry, Lily quickly wrapped the ankle and put on her lucky sneakers. There was no way she was missing the competition. Hobbling to the bathroom, she popped a couple aspirins, hoping the medicine would help with the pain. As she took the steps downstairs, the ankle gave out, and she tumbled down the rest of the steps. She cried out in pain. Suddenly, she sat straight up in bed. Her heart was racing, but thankfully, it had just been a bad dream. Still, she checked her ankle before going back to sleep.

### YOUR TURN

_____

_____

_____

_____

_____

_____

_____

# IT'S TIME FOR PARAGRAPH PRACTICE!

**Write a strong five-sentence *creative* paragraph that tells an action story.**

## Example paragraph:

Zach walked the grocery store aisles, searching for items on his mother's list. Suddenly, a man comes barreling down the same aisle, running as fast as he can. "Stop him!" The store manager cried. "He's a thief!" Not giving it another thought, Zach took his cart, and right when the man ran past him, Zach hurled the cart at the man. The thief tripped and fell face-first into an end display.

### YOUR TURN

_____

_____

_____

_____

_____

_____

_____

_____

# IT'S TIME FOR PARAGRAPH PRACTICE!

Write a strong five-sentence *creative* paragraph that tells a science fiction story.

## Example paragraph:

Roger joined the military police on his eighteenth birthday. All the other young men were joining, and Roger didn't want to be left out. It's not everyday that the government sends forces to Mars to fight the unsuspected aliens that had arrived and had turned out to be hostile. Just the same, as Roger made his way through the house, he felt sad at the thought of leaving. He had signed up for a two-year mission. His younger sister would be fourteen when he returned...if he returned. But he didn't want to think about that. He had already said his good-byes, but his family still waited for him at the door. "Are you ready, son?" his father asked, trying not to get emotional. Roger picked up his bag and nodded. In five days' time, he would be on another planet, far away from his family.

### YOUR TURN

_____

_____

_____

_____

_____

_____

_____

# IT'S TIME FOR PARAGRAPH PRACTICE!

**Write a strong five-sentence *creative* paragraph that tells a funny story.**

## Example paragraph:

Sally should not have drunk the soda. Cheerleading and soda consumption did not mix well. But the bell had rung, which meant the pep assembly would begin shortly. She hurriedly changed in her uniform and ran to where the cheer team was waiting. She felt the bubbles rise, and she hid, as best she could, a burp. "You all right?" Lexi asked. Sally smiled and said she was fine. Then the pep assembly began. Piles of students found their places on the bleachers. And right as everyone quieted down and before Principal Jones began to speak, Sally could no longer contain it. Her burp was loud and long and filled the whole gymnasium. There was a pause before everyone began to laugh.

## YOUR TURN

_____

_____

_____

_____

_____

_____

_____

_____

# IT'S TIME FOR PARAGRAPH PRACTICE!

**Creative Paragraph Writing is FUN!**

Write a five-sentence *creative* paragraph of YOUR CHOICE that tells your own

original story.

**YOUR TURN**

---

---

---

---

---

---

---

---

---

---

---

# IT'S TIME FOR PARAGRAPH PRACTICE!

**Creative Paragraph Writing is FUN!**

Write a five-sentence *creative* paragraph of YOUR CHOICE that tells your own original story.

**YOUR TURN**

_____

_____

_____

_____

_____

_____

_____

_____

_____

_____

_____

_____

# IT'S TIME FOR PARAGRAPH PRACTICE!

**Creative Paragraph Writing is FUN!**

Write a five-sentence *creative* paragraph of YOUR CHOICE that tells your own

original story.

**YOUR TURN**

_____

_____

_____

_____

_____

_____

_____

_____

_____

_____

_____

# PARAGRAPH PRACTICE:

# READER RESPONSE

# IT'S TIME FOR PARAGRAPH PRACTICE!

Reader Response: Read the selection below and complete the paragraph responses following it.

### Dear Grandmother

Dear Grandmother,

If you are receiving this letter, then we are well on our way to the Americas and the New World! Father promises that we will start a new life and will not want for food again. He has told us of new fruit trees and plenty of land to grow crops. These crops have not been tainted by the fungus and plague found in Ireland. I am tired of being constantly hungry, and I look forward to the day I can eat a warm meal for breakfast and dinner.

I pray once we are settled that you will join us. The passage to the Americas is rough, but struggle builds character. We met a sailor who will be aboard our ship, and he warned us to prepare for rough seas and cold winds. Father is undeterred and encourages us to brave the ship and to brave the new world.

My next letter will be sent when we stand upon the ground of the New World.

Sincerely,

Joseph

## Paragraph Practice:

In a paragraph, discuss what Joseph's family may endure while taking a ship from Ireland to the Americas. What do they need to bring to prepare for such a trip?

_____

_____

_____

_____

_____

## Paragraph Practice:

Writing letters are a great way to be expressive in our writing and to share our world with

someone else. Write a letter to someone you love (a parent, grandparent, friend, etc.).

Write about your day or anything new about your life.

Dear _____,

I have so much to tell you!

_____

_____

_____

_____

_____

_____

_____

Sincerely,

_____

# IT'S TIME FOR PARAGRAPH PRACTICE!

Reader Response: Read the selection below and complete the paragraph responses following it.

## *Penguins*

The penguin is a bird, but it does not fly. Penguins are not like other birds. They are unique birds, and although they do have feathers, even their feathers are unusual. Other birds have rows of feathers that grow in a specific pattern. A penguin's feathers grow all over, like hair on a mammal.

You will not see penguins in the air, and you will not see them in trees. You will see them in the water, in fact you will see them below the surface of the water if you have an underwater video camera. The penguin is an ocean bird, living in and near the ocean. While the penguin is not a great flier as the eagle is, the penguin can out-swim most birds and can probably out-swim some other aquatic animals. The penguin has thick strong wings and flippers instead of feet that it uses to push through the water.

When the penguin is on land, it walks along slowly, and this limited mobility may be one reason the penguin spends more time in the water. The penguin's food source is in the water, the fish it catches. They have solid bones, while other birds have bones that are not solid.

# Paragraph Practice:

In one paragraph, discuss how penguins are different than other birds.

_____

_____

_____

_____

_____

# Paragraph Practice:

Would you rather be a penguin or an eagle? In a paragraph, explain why.

_____

_____

_____

_____

_____

# IT'S TIME FOR PARAGRAPH PRACTICE!

Reader Response: Read the selection below and complete the paragraph responses following it.

### Traveling West

Long ago, when people settled the United States, most lived in the East, and it was hard to travel west. There were no planes, trains, or automobiles. People traveled by wagon or boat, and it took many days to reach their destination.

Although it was difficult, in the 1840s, many people traveled far across the United States from the East to the West. They were pioneers. They would settle in the western part of the country after a challenging journey to a new life. People traveled in groups, and each family would buy a covered wagon, which is a big wooden wagon with a kind of tent on it.

In the next century, people built a railroad that crossed the United States. By 1900, there were many more people in the West, and thousands of people came west by train. A trip that had taken months now took passengers a few days of comfortable transit. The railroad brought many changes, and the pioneers became legends as the country developed into the nation of today.

## Paragraph Practice:

In a paragraph, describe the difficulties in traveling by wagon from the east to the west. What would be the challenges? What would be the dangers?

_____

_____

_____

_____

_____

_____

## Paragraph Practice:

If you had to take a trip today all the way to California with your family (in a car), what would you take with you? How is it similar and/or different to what pioneer children might have taken with them?

_____

_____

_____

_____

_____

# IT'S TIME FOR PARAGRAPH PRACTICE!

Reader Response: Read the selection below and complete the paragraph responses following it.

## Food Scientists

The more you know about plants and foods, the healthier you will be. Food scientists have a lot to do with what we know about plants and the food we eat. For example, some foods can provide you with essential vitamins to keep you healthy, but some foods can make you sick. It is very important to know how to distinguish between the two. You also need to learn how to keep food safe and prevent it from spoiling. There's so much to learn. There is also a lot to learn about how to grow plants and how to prepare them for eating. Food Scientists help us in all these areas so that we can enjoy food and be healthy!

It's a good thing we have food scientists to help us stay safe. These scientists are people who have careers learning about plants and food. They conduct experiments and observe the different plants and food to understand how they benefit us and to learn how to make them grow better. They study how to keep them safe, which in turn helps people live healthier lives.

# Paragraph Practice:

In a paragraph explain why scientists are needed to help us understand the food we eat. Based on the reading, what do they do? What can you infer about them? What would happen without scientists?

_____

_____

_____

_____

_____

# Paragraph Practice:

In a paragraph describe the healthy plants that you like to eat (plants are anything that grows from the ground, including fruits and vegetables). Why is it important to eat these healthy plants?

_____

_____

_____

_____

_____

# IT'S TIME FOR PARAGRAPH PRACTICE!

Reader Response: Read the poetry selection below and complete the paragraph responses following it.

### *"Masks"*

*We wear them everyday*

*We hide our identity*

*We pretend*

*We imagine*

*We hide*

*But...*

*What if we took them off?*

*What if we learned to be ourselves?*

*Would we find others like us?*

*But...*

*We feel safer with them on*

*We feel less exposed*

*We feel tucked away*

*So, we leave our masks in place.*

## Paragraph Practice:

This poem is about not hiding who you are. What is something about yourself that is fun to know? Were you born in another country? Are you double-jointed? Can you make people laugh? Think about some fun things about your authentic self and share them in a paragraph.

---

---

---

---

---

## Paragraph Practice:

In a paragraph, discuss why this poem is sad. Why is it important to be your true self and not to pretend to be someone you're not?

---

---

---

---

---

# IT'S TIME FOR PARAGRAPH PRACTICE!

Reader Response: Read the selection below and complete the paragraph responses following it.

### A Country Mouse in the Big City

### (A Retelling of Aesop's fable: A Town Mouse and A Country Mouse)

Matty the country mouse invited his cousin, Cyrus the city mouse, to come visit him. Matty lived on the outskirts of Farmer Fred's fields. When Cyrus agreed to visit, Matty was excited. His cleaned his home at the bottom of Farmer Fred's large oak tree. He swept the floors and washed his blankets. He foraged and found delicious acorns. He searched the fields and found fallen corn kernels. Matty had baskets full.

When Cyrus arrived, Matty marveled at his cousin's fancy clothes. Matty was merely a country mouse and didn't wear city clothes.

"Is this where you live?" Cyrus asked. "This hole in the tree is so small."

"I like it," Matty said. "It's comfortable and warm."

Cyrus stepped outside. "Your view is of corn fields. I have a view of the whole city and its beautiful lights."

"I like the corn fields. They keep me fed. At night, I don't need the city lights because I have the stars in the sky to admire."

When they sat down for supper, Cyrus frowned. "Is this all you have to eat? Corn and acorns? You should visit me in the city. There is so much food to choose from!"

Matty thought about it. He enjoyed the country, but maybe Cyrus was right. Maybe the city had more to offer him. "I would like to visit the city. I've never been there."

After Cyrus's visit, Matty packed a bag and traveled to the big city. There was concrete and large buildings, but Matty didn't see many trees or fields. "We don't need them here," Cyrus said. "City living is fast living."

Cyrus took Matty to a restaurant. It had a dumpster full of leftover food. Matty had never seen so much food! Afterward, Matty noticed a small contraption outside the restaurant's back door. "Don't touch that," Cyrus warned. "It's a mouse trap."

"A mouse trap?" Matty was surprised. There were no traps out in the country.

"Well?" Cyrus asked at the end of Matty's visit. "How do you like the city? You can come live with me. We could live the high life! There is always something to do and plenty of food to eat."

"I like country living," Matty confessed. "I like quiet nights and big skies. I like my little hole in the oak tree."

So, Cyrus and Matty said goodbye, each promising to visit the other.

# Paragraph Practice:

Matty liked living in the country, but Cyrus liked living in the city. Would you prefer country living or city living? Write a paragraph that explains your answer.

_____

_____

_____

_____

_____

# Paragraph Practice:

This fable is about the importance of being thankful for what you have and not comparing your life with others. Write a paragraph about things you want versus what you already have. What are some ways you stay thankful for what you have?

_____

_____

_____

_____

_____

# IT'S TIME FOR PARAGRAPH PRACTICE!

Reader Response: Read the selection below and complete the paragraph responses following it.

## *The Elves and the Shoemaker*

## (a retelling of the fairytale by the Brothers Grimm)

There once was an old shoemaker and his wife. They were poor, and no one needed new shoes. They could barely afford food let alone any materials to make new shoes. One night, the sad shoemaker had one piece of leather left to make shoes, but it wasn't enough. He said his prayers and fell asleep.

When he woke up, he saw a beautiful pair of leather shoes. He was astonished and set them out in his shop's window. In no time, a customer came and bought the shoes for an extravagant price. The shoemaker took the money and bought more leather. Sure enough, when he woke up the next morning, a new pair of shoes awaited him. This happened over and over until the shoemaker and his wife were quite prosperous.

One evening, close to Christmas, the shoemaker and his wife decided to stay up and see just who it was that kept blessing them with new shoes. They hid behind a door and in the dark of night, they saw three little elves sneak inside and begin to work together quickly on the shoes. By the end of night, the new shoes were complete, and the elves ran off before the morning light.

"We must do something for them," the wife said. "Did you see their bare feet and shivering bodies. Let us make warm clothes and shoes for them."

So, that is exactly what the shoemaker and his wife did. While the shoemaker made little pairs of shoes for the elves, the wife made them warm clothes. They left them out and watched as the elves came back and saw their gift. The elves were overjoyed and put on the clothes and shoes, then they danced in happiness and left the shoemaker's shop. They did not return, but the shoemaker and his wife were wealthy for the rest of their lives.

## Paragraph Practice:

This story is about the importance of blessing others. In a paragraph, discuss how the elves were blessings to the shoemaker and his wife, and how the shoemaker and his wife were blessings to the elves.

_____

_____

_____

_____

_____

## Paragraph Practice:

In a paragraph write about a time you were a blessing to someone else. Or write about how you could be a blessing in the future.

# PARAGRAPH PRACTICE:

# YOUR CHOICE!

## PRACTICE PARAGRAPHS IN YOUR OWN WAY

# IT'S TIME FOR PARAGRAPH PRACTICE!

This section is designed for you to practice paragraph writing on your own. Choose any topic and write one paragraph about it.

***Here are some ideas:*** Write about your family, or your pets, or your friends. Write about the things you like to do or your favorite memories. Write about your goals and dreams and how you plan to accomplish them. Write about your favorite movie or game.

**YOUR TURN**

_____

_____

_____

_____

_____

**YOUR TURN**

_____

_____

_____

_____

_____

# IT'S TIME FOR PARAGRAPH PRACTICE!

This section is designed for you to practice paragraph writing on your own. Choose any topic and write one paragraph about it.

*Here are some ideas:* Write about your family, or your pets, or your friends. Write about the things you like to do or your favorite memories. Write about your goals and dreams and how you plan to accomplish them. Write about your favorite movie or game.

## YOUR TURN

_____

_____

_____

_____

_____

_____

## YOUR TURN

_____

_____

_____

_____

_____

_____

# IT'S TIME FOR PARAGRAPH PRACTICE!

This section is designed for you to practice paragraph writing on your own. Choose any topic and write one paragraph about it.

*Here are some ideas:* Write about your family, or your pets, or your friends. Write about the things you like to do or your favorite memories. Write about your goals and dreams and how you plan to accomplish them. Write about your favorite movie or game.

## YOUR TURN

_____

_____

_____

_____

_____

## YOUR TURN

_____

_____

_____

_____

_____

# PARAGRAPH PRACTICE: PARAGRAPH EDITING

# PARAGRAPH PRACTICE: EDITING

**Directions:**
Please read through the paragraph below, and then fix the grammar and punctuation errors. Once the edits are completed, please rewrite the paragraph correctly, implementing the proper edits into the rewrite.
*Can you find and fix the 1) capitalization errors, 2) punctuation errors, and 3) spelling errors?*

## Paragraph:

Did you know that the equater is the longest latitude line it is about 25000 miles long that's really long it is right in the middle of our planit, equal distance from the north pole and south poll this latitude line crosses into 14 different countries most places along the equater have equal parts day and night

## PARAGRAPH REWRITE

_____

_____

_____

_____

_____

_____

# PARAGRAPH PRACTICE: EDITING

**Directions:**
Please read through the paragraph below, and then fix the grammar and punctuation errors. Once the edits are completed, please rewrite the paragraph correctly, implementing the proper edits into the rewrite.
*Can you find and fix the 1) capitalization errors, 2) punctuation errors, and 3) spelling errors?*

## Paragraph:

most of the land along the equater is warm and tropicul but not everywhere there are rainy seasons in these places did u know that there is a place along the equater that even gets snow it is the volcan cayambe in the country of ecuador it is these mountain slopes that get snow so not every place along the equater is warm and tropicul

## PARAGRAPH REWRITE

_____

_____

_____

_____

_____

_____

# PARAGRAPH PRACTICE: EDITING

**Directions:**
Please read through the paragraph below, and then fix the grammar and punctuation errors. Once the edits are completed, please rewrite the paragraph correctly, implementing the proper edits into the rewrite.
*Can you find and fix the 1) capitalization errors, 2) comma errors, and 3) spelling errors?*

## Paragraph:

According to u.s. news and world report their our some top vacation locations. In america the place that tops the list is the grand canyon. In europe france is the top vacation destination. Most vacationers want to see sights and have adventures but many also want to vacation in warm sunny climits.

## PARAGRAPH REWRITE

_____

_____

_____

_____

_____

_____

# PARAGRAPH PRACTICE: EDITING

**Directions:**
Please read through the paragraph below, and then fix the grammar and punctuation errors. Once the edits are completed, please rewrite the paragraph correctly, implementing the proper edits into the rewrite.
*Can you find and fix the 1) there, their, and they're errors, 2) comma errors, and 3) spelling errors?*

## Paragraph:

Just a decade ago most young people started there first job at sixteen years old. Today it is different because the average young person is wating to get a job until 18 years old. They're are several reasons for this. For example young people are being taken care of by parents and there immediate needs our being met. Their is no need to work in they're opinion.

## PARAGRAPH REWRITE

_____

_____

_____

_____

_____

_____

_____

# PARAGRAPH PRACTICE: EDITING

**Directions:**
Please read through the paragraph below, and then fix the grammar and punctuation errors. Once the edits are completed, please rewrite the paragraph correctly, implementing the proper edits into the rewrite.
*Can you find and fix the 1) there, their, and they're errors, 2) your and you're errors, and 3) apostrophe errors?*

## Paragraph:

If you are wanting to earn money, your not alone. Their are many reason's to want extra cash. Young peoples' reason's may differ than older people's reasons. For example, if your a young person, you might not need to worry about house and car payments. This doesn't mean that your not in need of funds. They're numerous reasons for young people to need cash: such as to start saving's accounts and to pay for extracurricular activies'.

## PARAGRAPH REWRITE

_____

_____

_____

_____

_____

# PARAGRAPH PRACTICE: EDITING

**Directions:**
Please read through the paragraph below, and then fix the grammar and punctuation errors. Once the edits are completed, please rewrite the paragraph correctly, implementing the proper edits into the rewrite.
*Can you find and fix the 1) comma errors, 2) apostrophe errors, and 3) spelling errors?*

## Paragraph:

Dolphins' are underwater treasures and are highly intellugent. They live in fresh and salt water and they make a variety of sound's as a form of comunicashun. Unfortunately marine traffic along coastal towns has created to much noise. This affect's dolphin's because they are unable to comunicate to those in there pod.

## PARAGRAPH REWRITE

_____

_____

_____

_____

_____

_____

# PARAGRAPH PRACTICE: EDITING

**Directions:**

Please read through the paragraph below, and then fix the grammar and punctuation errors. Once the edits are completed, please rewrite the paragraph correctly, implementing the proper edits into the rewrite.

*Can you find and fix the 1) capitalization errors, 2) punctuation errors, and 3) word choice errors.*

## Paragraph:

Camping with my family is the best thing ever we always go on super cool trips like camping at the beach and one time we camped at mt rushmore when we camp we sleep in a tent and build bonfires and fish at the lake and cook over the open flame we don't like to camp when its to cold so we camp in the summer. its my favorite thing to do i cant wait to do it again.

## PARAGRAPH REWRITE

_____

_____

_____

_____

_____

_____

_____

# PARAGRAPH PRACTICE: EDITING

**Directions:**

Please read through the paragraph below, and then fix the grammar and punctuation errors. Once the edits are completed, please rewrite the paragraph correctly, implementing the proper edits into the rewrite.

*Can you find and fix the 1) capitalization errors, 2) punctuation errors, and 3) spelling errors?*

## Paragraph:

ive been fishing with my grandpa since i was for years old he has a pond near his house and we will go to the dock with our fishing poles some worms and a cooler full of sodas and sit and fish grandpa says that fishing in the morning is best becuse that's when the fish bite sometimes he wakes me up really early and im grouchy but once i get to the pond im hapy to be there.

## PARAGRAPH REWRITE

_____

_____

_____

_____

_____

_____

—

# PARAGRAPH PRACTICE: EDITING

**Directions:**
Please read through the paragraph below, and then fix the grammar and punctuation errors. Once the edits are completed, please rewrite the paragraph correctly, implementing the proper edits into the rewrite.
*Can you find and fix the 1) capitalization errors, 2) comma errors, and 3) spelling errors?*

## Paragraph:

fireflies light up the summer nites but what makes them specil is more than just there glow for example fireflies don't live very long lives after they mate they are done living  also they are not known to do a lot of eating this might be becuse they don't live long  they need moist enviroments and warm climits which is why we see them in the summer and near the trees and forests.

## PARAGRAPH REWRITE

_____

_____

_____

_____

_____

_____

# PARAGRAPH PRACTICE: EDITING

**Directions:**
Please read through the paragraph below, and then fix the grammar and punctuation errors. Once the edits are completed, please rewrite the paragraph correctly, implementing the proper edits into the rewrite.

*Can you find and fix the 1) punctuation errors, 2) comma errors, and 3) spelling errors?*

## Paragraph:

Autum is my favorit season because i like the cool whether and the pretty coloerd leaves and the pumpkin patches and apples to pick. One time me and my family went on a hayrie and picked pumpkins and drank cider and ate hot doughnuts that was one of my best days ever and its why i love fall or autum so much.

## PARAGRAPH REWRITE

_____

_____

_____

_____

_____

_____

_____

# PARAGRAPH PRACTICE: EDITING

**Directions:**

Please read through the paragraph below, and then fix the grammar and punctuation errors. Once the edits are completed, please rewrite the paragraph correctly, implementing the proper edits into the rewrite.

*Can you find and fix the 1) there, their, and they're errors, 2) punctuation errors, and 3) apostrophe errors?*

## Paragraph:

Farm life is not an easy life you have to get up before the sun comes up so you can take care of the animals. They need to eat before you do and there needs come first Some need they're exercise and some like cows need to be milked this takes a lot of time and its first thing in the morning it might not seem fare but thats why farm life isn't easy.

## PARAGRAPH REWRITE

_____

_____

_____

_____

_____

_____

# PARAGRAPH PRACTICE: EDITING

**Directions:**
Please read through the paragraph below, and then fix the grammar and punctuation errors. Once the edits are completed, please rewrite the paragraph correctly, implementing the proper edits into the rewrite.
*Can you find and fix the 1) punctuation errors, 2) apostrophe errors, and 3) spelling errors?*

## Paragraph:

video games are exciting and challenging for children some don't think there

good and children shouldn't play them research shows that video games can be

appropriate and challenign in a good way. They help with brain activity and hand to eye

coordination as long as children don't play inappropriate games they should be able to

enjoy a video game during they're down time.

### PARAGRAPH REWRITE

_____

_____

_____

_____

_____

_____

# PARAGRAPH PRACTICE: MINI-ESSAYS

# LET'S GET BUILDING!

## The Two-Paragraph Mini-Essay

**Directions:**

*Problem solve:* Choose a newspaper or online article about an important current event that can be seen as problematic. Read it carefully, then write two paragraphs that discuss solutions to solve the "problem" or "challenge."

## Step 1: Find a current article about an important current event that can be seen as problematic.

1. What is the article title that you chose?

   _____

   _____

2. Who is the author?

   _____

3. What is the website or news source?

   _____

   _____

4. What year/date was the article written?

   _____

## Step 2: Please write a summary of what the article is about.

_____

_____

_____

**Step 3: Please write two paragraphs that help "problem solve" the issue this article addresses.**

**Paragraph One:** My first solution to this problem is...

_____

_____

_____

_____

_____

_____

_____

_____**Paragraph Two:** My second solution to this problem is...

_____

_____

_____

_____

_____

**Step 4:** Once these two paragraphs are drafted, please type them up, fixing any errors. This is your final mini-essay! Great job!

# LET'S GET BUILDING!

### The Two-Paragraph Mini-Essay

**Directions:**
*Information about Systems:* Choose two newspaper or online articles about an important "system" that helps sustain us. Some examples include farming, shipping, highways and infrastructure, public education, etc. Read the articles, then write two paragraphs that inform the reader about the "system" and why it is important.

## Step 1: Find two articles about a "system" that helps sustain us.

1. **What is the article title # 1 that you chose?**

   _____

   _____

2. **Who is the author?**

   _____

3. **What is the website or news source?**

   _____

   _____

4. **What year/date was the article written?**

   _____

5. **What is the second article title that you chose?**

   _____

   _____

6. Who is the author?

_____

7. What is the website or news source?

_____

_____

8. What year/date was the article written?

_____

# Step 2: Please write a summary of what the articles are about.

_____

_____

_____

# Step 3: Please write two paragraphs that inform the reader about the "system" that helps us live the way we do.

**Paragraph One:** Let me discuss how the "system" works...

_____

_____

_____

_____

_____

_____

_____

_____

_____

_____

_____**Paragraph Two:** This paragraph will discuss why the "system" is

important...

_____

_____

_____

_____

_____

_____

_____

_____

_____

_____

**Step 4: Once these two paragraphs are drafted, please type them up, fixing any errors. This is your final mini-essay! Great job!**

# LET'S GET BUILDING!

## The Three-Paragraph Mini-Essay

**Directions:**

*Read and Respond*: Choose a book and write a three paragraph response to the book. Here are some sample paragraph topics for you to choose from:

- *What were the main themes or ideas of the book?* (For example, was the book about friendship? Was it about the importance of family or believing in yourself?) Make sure to provide evidence from the book to prove your point.
- *Describe the protagonist in the book (the main character).* What are they like? How did they change or grow from start to finish? What lesson did they learn?
- *Describe the antagonist in the book (the character that causes the conflict).* What are they/it like? Did they/it learn their lesson and change?
- *Was there someone or something from the book that fascinated you*? What was it that interested you? Describe them or the event and why it intrigued you.
- *Place yourself in the book.* Would you do anything differently?

## Step 1: Read the book selection.

1. **What is the book title that you chose?**

   _____

   _____

2. **Who is the author?**

   _____

3. **What year/date was the book written?**

   _____

**Step 2: Please write a summary of what the book is about.**

_____

_____

_____

_____

_____

_____

_____

**Step 3: Create a list of characters and briefly describe them.**

Character #1:

_____

_____

Character #2:

_____

_____

Character #3:

_____

_____

Character #4:

_____

_____

Character #5:

_____

_____

**Step 4: Please write three paragraphs that respond to the book. Use the example topics to help you get started.**

**Paragraph One:** What I found most interesting about the book was ...

_____

_____

_____

_____

_____

_____

_____

_____**Paragraph Two:** If I inserted myself into the story, I would have done

things much differently...

_____

_____

_____

_____

_____

_____

**Paragraph Three:** There were some important themes in this book...

_____

_____

_____

_____

_____

_____

**Step 5: Once these two paragraphs are drafted, please type them up, fixing any errors. This is your final mini-essay! Great job!**

# PARAGRAPH PRACTICE IS COMPLETE!

Consider Other Late November Learning Tree Titles:

## Journaling for Kids

## Journaling is Writing Too!

## Journaling through Scripture for Teens

## Practicing Poetry

www.ingramcontent.com/pod-product-compliance
Lightning Source LLC
Chambersburg PA
CBHW080846120626
46553CB00009B/2589